I0140075

The Lord gave this message to Jonah son of Amittai:

2 "Get up and go to the great city of Nineveh. Announce my judgment against it because I have seen how wicked its people are."

3 But Jonah got up and went in the opposite direction to get away from the Lord. He went down to the port of Joppa, where he found a ship leaving for Tarshish. He bought a ticket and went on board, hoping to escape from the Lord by sailing to Tarshish.

Jonah 1:1-3

ONE BOOK
OF
JONAH
IS ENOUGH

Books by Tim Barker

ONE BOOK
OF
JONAH
IS ENOUGH

Tim R. Barker, D. Min.

Network Pastor/Superintendent
South Texas Ministry Network

ONE BOOK OF JONAH IS ENOUGH
By Tim Barker

1st ed.

Scriptures taken from the Holy Bible, New International Version®, NIV®. Copyright © 1973, 1978, 1984, 2011 by Biblica, Inc.™ Used by permission of Zondervan. All rights reserved worldwide. www.zondervan.com The "NIV" and "New International Version" are trademarks registered in the United States Patent and Trademark Office by Biblica, Inc.™.

This book and its contents are wholly the creation and intellectual property of Tim Barker.

This book may not be reproduced in whole or in part, by electronic process or any other means, without written permission of the author.

ISBN: 979-8-9924875-9-6

Copyright © 2026 by Tim Barker

All Rights Reserved

DEDICATION

At a pivotal moment in his transition, my predecessor, Superintendent Joseph P. Granberry, made a statement that has lingered with me ever since. As he prayerfully considered retirement, he offered this simple yet weighty counsel: "Stay in God's will for your life—because one Book of Jonah is enough."

I took note of his words and was drawn back to Scripture. I revisited a familiar story—one my childhood Sunday School teachers once brought to life with a flannel graph. But this time, the passage spoke differently. The Holy Spirit illuminated the text with fresh clarity:

"But Jonah arose to flee to Tarshish from the presence of the Lord. He went down to Joppa, found a ship going to Tarshish; so he paid the fare and went down into it, to go with them to Tarshish from the presence of the Lord."

Suddenly, the insight was unmistakable.

When Jonah ran from the will of God, Jonah

paid.

He paid the fare to board the ship.

He paid the cost of three days in a giant fish.

He paid the consequences of a desert experience in his life.

But when Jonah finally aligned himself with the will of God, God paid.

This is a truth every leader eventually learns: Running from God's will always comes with a price tag.

Walking in God's will releases divine provision.

You can pay to get where you want to go, or you can obey and allow God to fund where He is sending you.

And truly—one Book of Jonah is enough.

More recently, my coworkers and dear friends, Don Wiehe and Beth Wiehe, have navigated their own season of transition with grace, wisdom, and integrity, setting an example worthy of imitation.

Therefore, it is with deep gratitude and respect that I dedicate this book to Rev. Joseph P. Granberry and to Pastors Don and Beth Wiehe.

PREFACE

This book is a prophetic, pastoral, and practical wake-up call:

God is patient—but He is not interested in giving you *Jonah, Volume 2.*

One Book of Jonah is enough.

The message of Jonah is not about a fish.

It's about delayed obedience, selective compassion, wounded prophets, reluctant servants, and the mercy of God that outpaces human comfort.

This book is written for:

- *Leaders* who know God's voice but wrestle with His assignments
- *Believers* who love God but struggle with people
- *Ministers* who obey outwardly but resist inwardly
- *Churches* who want revival without repentance

- *Anyone who suspects* God keeps repeating lessons because we keep dodging obedience
- *When God Repeats* Himself because we won't move
- *Lessons God Refuses* to teach twice
- *Delayed Obedience*, reluctant hearts, and the mercy that won't quit
- *Why God Won't Rewrite* what He's already spoken

God will repeat His message, extend His mercy, and pursue His servant—but He will not rewrite the lesson.

One Book of Jonah is enough.

TABLE OF CONTENTS

INTRODUCTION

This book is about:

- What Jonah teaches every generation
- *Where God is still repeating Himself today*
- How to break the cycle and move forward

There are moments in life when you realize you've been here before.

- Same conversations—same tension
- *Same instructions—same resistance*
- Different year—same lesson

The problem isn't that God isn't speaking.

The problem is that He's already spoken.

The Book of Jonah is only four chapters long, yet it contains enough truth to last a lifetime. It is brief not because the lesson is small, but because it should not have to be repeated.

Jonah proves something uncomfortable:

- God can forgive rebellion—but He will not renegotiate obedience.
- *The Word came to Jonah.*
- Jonah ran.

But the Word came again. That alone should sober us.

If God has to say it twice, it's not because He was unclear the first time—*it's because we were unwilling to listen and do what He said.*

This book is not written to shame the runner. *It is written to awaken the sleeper.*

Because one Book of Jonah is enough.

Pastor Tim

YOU CAN OUTRUN THE CALL, BUT YOU CANNOT OUTRUN THE AUTHOR.

— 1 —

The Word Came
... Again

THE HIDDEN COST OF
RUNNING FROM GOD

Jonah 1:3 (NIV) proclaims:

*"But Jonah ran away from the Lord and
headed for Tarshish. He went down to
Joppa, where he found a ship bound for
that port. After paying the fare, he went
aboard and sailed for Tarshish to flee
from the Lord."*

The text does not waste words.

It does not say Jonah *almost* paid. It does not say *someone else* covered it.

It says Jonah paid the fare.

That detail is not accidental—it is theological.

WHEN YOU RUN, YOU PAY

Jonah is running from a divine assignment, and the first thing Scripture highlights is not the storm, not the fish, not Nineveh—

It's the bill.

Running from God always comes with a price tag.

You will pay in:

- Peace
- *Sleep*
- Clarity
- *Relationships*
- Momentum
- *Emotional energy*

- Spiritual authority

Disobedience is never free—it is self-funded rebellion.

- Jonah did not need a miracle to run.
- *He did not need favor.*
- He did not need provision.

All he needed was money ...

... and he had enough to finance his own disobedience.

The frightening thing is that God will often let you afford what will eventually destroy you.

PROVISION DOES NOT EQUAL PERMISSION

Jonah had the money. Jonah found the ship. Jonah boarded without resistance.

And that is where many people get confused.

"If God didn't want me to go, why did the door open?"

Because open doors do not always mean

approved directions.

Some doors open because God approves. Some doors open because God allows you to learn.

- Just because you can afford it doesn't mean it's God.
- *Just because it works doesn't mean it's right.*
- Just because it's available doesn't mean it's ordained.

Jonah's disobedience was fully funded.

GOD'S WILL IS PAID FOR BY GOD

Here is the contrast the Spirit wants us to see:

- Running from God: *Jonah paid the fare.*
- Obeying God: *God prepared the fish.*
- Preaching in Nineveh: *God prepared the people.*
- Jonah's shade: *God prepared the plant.*

Every time Jonah cooperates with God, God does the preparing.

If God orders it, God funds it.

When you walk in obedience:

- God pays the price.
- *God opens the door.*
- God sustains the assignment.
- *God covers the cost.*

But when you run—you'll pay.

- You'll pay emotionally.
- *You'll pay spiritually.*
- You'll pay relationally.
- *You'll pay internally.*

RUNNING ALWAYS TAKES YOU DOWN

Notice the repeated language in Jonah 1:3:

- He went down to Joppa.
- *He went down into the ship.*

Disobedience always descends.

You don't run from God and go up. You go down—in discernment, joy, clarity, and authority.

And here's the danger:

You can be going *down* while telling yourself you're "just taking a break."

THE HIDDEN COST OF TARSHISH

- Tarshish looked attractive.
- *Tarshish felt logical.*
- Tarshish was far away from Nineveh.
- *Tarshish seemed to be a better choice.*

But Tarshish came with:

- A fare
- *A storm*
- Innocent sailors at risk
- *Public exposure*
- Isolation
- *Confinement*

- Repentance under pressure

Jonah paid to run ...

... then paid again to repent.

Disobedience always charges interest.

WHEN GOD PAYS, HE PREPARES

The Bible repeatedly says, "The Lord prepared ..."

- A great fish
- *A gourd*
- A worm
- *A vehement east wind*

When Jonah finally aligns with God's will, heaven goes to work, because obedience activates divine preparation.

- You don't have to manipulate.
- *You don't have to force.*
- You don't have to fund it yourself.

If it's God's will—it's God's bill.

A PROPHETIC LINE FOR THE CHURCH

Some of us are exhausted not because the assignment is heavy—but because we're paying for something God never authorized.

- You're tired because you're financing Tarshish.
- *You're drained because you're funding delay.*
- You're weary because you're paying for what obedience would have covered.

God is saying:

> *"Stop paying for what I already promised to provide."*

CLOSING DECLARATION:

If I'm running—I'll pay. If I'm obedient—He'll pay.

- I don't want self-funded rebellion.
- I want heaven-backed obedience.

Because one Book of Jonah is enough.

Tarshish Looks Like Self-Care

(BUT YOU'LL PAY FOR IT)

Jonah 1:3 (NIV) reveals the prophet abandoning God's mission:

> *"But Jonah ran away from the Lord and headed for Tarshish. He went down to Joppa, where he found a ship bound for that port. After paying the fare, he went aboard and sailed for Tarshish to flee from the Lord."*

RUNNING RARELY LOOKS REBELLIOUS

Jonah did not run in anger.

- He did not curse God.
- He did not announce his rebellion.

He simply changed direction.

And that is how disobedience most often appears—not loud, not dramatic, but *reasonable.*

- Tarshish looked peaceful.
- *Tarshish looked far enough away.*
- Tarshish looked like relief.

Today we would call it:

- Needing space
- *Protecting my mental health*
- Taking a season off
- *Stepping back for clarity*

But the Bible calls it what it is:

Fleeing from the presence of the Lord.

THE DETAIL HEAVEN REFUSES
TO SKIP

Scripture is economical with words—so when it adds a detail, it is intentional.

"After paying the fare, he went aboard ..."

This is not a travel note ...

... this is a spiritual law.

When Jonah ran from God's will, *he paid.*

- God did not pay for Jonah's disobedience.
- *Grace did not subsidize rebellion.*
- Mercy did not underwrite escape.

Jonah reached into his own pocket and financed his own delay.

Running from God is always self-funded.

IF YOU RUN, YOU'LL PAY

Jonah paid money—but that was just the beginning.

He would later pay with:

- Peace
- *Sleep*
- Credibility
- *Public exposure*
- Isolation
- *Confinement*
- Deep repentance

Disobedience always sends an invoice.

You may not see it immediately. You may think you can afford it. But eventually the cost comes due.

And here is the uncomfortable truth:

- *God will often allow you to afford what He never approved.*
- *Provision does not equal permission.*

OPEN DOORS CAN LEAD THE WRONG DIRECTION

Jonah found a ship already going where he wanted to go.

- No resistance
- *No warning sign*
- No closed door

That's dangerous.

Because we often assume: "If God didn't want me to go, He would stop me."

But sometimes God lets you go—*not to endorse your direction, but to expose your heart.*

- Some doors open because *God ordained them.*
- Some doors open because *you insisted.*

Jonah's Tarshish door was wide open—but heaven was not in it.

GOD'S WILL IS ALWAYS GOD-FUNDED

Watch the contrast as the story unfolds.

- When Jonah runs: *Jonah pays.*
- When Jonah surrenders: *God*

prepares.

The Lord prepared:

- A great fish
- *A city ready to repent*
- A plant for shade
- *A worm to correct*
- A wind to teach

When Jonah is in God's will, heaven goes to work.

If God orders it, God covers it.

Obedience does not mean it will be easy—but it does mean you *won't be paying for it alone.*

RUNNING ALWAYS TAKES YOU DOWN

Notice the language of descent:

- Jonah went *down* to Joppa.
- Jonah went *down* into the ship.
- Jonah later goes *down* into the sea.

Disobedience always moves downward.

- You don't drift upward.
- *You don't fall into obedience.*
- You descend when you run.

And what makes this so dangerous is that Jonah was asleep—

> *comfortable ...*
>
> > *resting ...*

—while going down.

TARSHISH IS EXPENSIVE

Tarshish cost Jonah more than Nineveh ever would have.

Nineveh required obedience.

Tarshish required payment.

Nineveh required trust.

Tarshish required financing.

Nineveh would have stretched Jonah.

Tarshish nearly destroyed him.

Disobedience is always more expensive than obedience.

A WORD FOR LEADERS

Some leaders are exhausted not because God gave them too much ...

> ... *but because they are paying for assignments God never assigned.*

- You're tired because you're *funding avoidance.*
- You're weary because you're *underwriting delay.*
- You're burned out because you're *paying for Tarshish.*

God is saying:

> *"If you'll stop paying for what I never sent you to do, I'll start providing for what I did."*

A LINE WORTH REMEMBERING:

When I run—I pay. When I obey—He pays.

- I don't want self-funded rebellion.
- I want heaven-backed obedience.

Because one Book of Jonah is enough.

Storms That Won't Let You Sleep

STORMS ARE NOT ALWAYS PUNISHMENT

Jonah 1:4–6 (NIV) gives us what happened next:

"Then the Lord sent a great wind on the sea, and such a violent storm arose that the ship threatened to break up. 5 All the sailors were afraid and each cried out to his own god. And they threw the cargo

into the sea to lighten the ship.

"But Jonah had gone below deck,
where he lay down and fell into a deep
sleep. ⁶ The captain went to him and said,
'How can you sleep? Get up and call on
your god! Maybe he will take notice of us
so that we will not perish.'"

NOT EVERY STORM IS THE DEVIL

One of the most dangerous misunderstand-ings in modern faith is assuming that every storm is satanic.

But the Bible is clear:

"The LORD sent out a great wind
into the sea."

This storm did not come from hell. It came

from heaven.

Not to destroy Jonah—but to interrupt him.

- Some storms are not attacks; *they are assignments.*
- Some turbulence is not opposition; *it is correction.*
- Some shaking is not judgment; *it is mercy with teeth.*

God loved Jonah too much to let Tarshish be peaceful.

THE STORM WAS LOUD— JONAH WAS SILENT

While the storm raged, Jonah slept.

- The wind was violent.
- *The sea was raging.*
- The ship was breaking apart.

And Jonah was unconscious.

Disobedience has a numbing effect.

- You can be in danger and not feel it.

- *You can be out of position and still be comfortable.*
- You can be asleep while everything around you is unraveling.

That's how deception works.

The greatest danger is not the storm—it's sleeping through it.

WHEN LEADERS SLEEP, OTHERS PANIC

The sailors were terrified. They were throwing cargo overboard. They were praying to every god they knew.

But Jonah—the man of God—was snoring.

Here is the sobering truth: *Jonah's disobedience endangered people who never heard God's command.*

Running from God never stays personal.

- Your delay affects your family.
- *Your avoidance affects your team.*

- Your silence affects your church.

Your rebellion creates storms others must survive.

Disobedience always spills over.

PAGANS WERE PRAYING—THE PROPHET WASN'T

The sailors prayed ...

    ... while Jonah slept.

That reversal should trouble us.

When unbelievers cry out for help and believers are disengaged, something is deeply wrong.

The captain had to wake the prophet and say:

"What meanest thou, O sleeper? arise, call upon thy God."

Imagine that ...

    ... a pagan preaching revival to a

prophet.

When the world must wake the church, the church has fallen asleep at the wrong time.

STORMS EXPOSE WHAT
SILENCE HIDES

Jonah could ignore God on land. But he could not silence God at sea.

The storm exposed what Jonah's comfort concealed.

God will allow pressure to reveal what peace permitted you to avoid.

Storms strip away:

- Pretending
- *Excuses*
- Half-truths
- *Spiritual apathy*

And they force a question: *Who is responsible for this storm?*

GOD WILL NOT LET YOU SINK QUIETLY

Notice this:

- God could have let Jonah reach Tarshish.
- *God could have let Jonah disobey quietly.*
- God could have let Jonah succeed at running.

But God loves too much to let His servants disappear without confrontation.

God will disrupt your comfort to preserve your calling.

The storm was loud because Jonah refused to listen when God spoke softly.

A WORD FOR THE CHURCH

Some storms are not because the church is under attack ...

... but because the church is out of alignment.

- God shakes what He loves.
- *God confronts what He calls.*
- God interrupts what threatens destiny.

The storm is not proof God is absent. It is often proof *He is present and unwilling to let you drift.*

THE WAKE-UP CALL

The captain didn't say: *"Figure this out later."*

He said: *"Arise. Call upon thy God."*

Storms demand a response.
- *Delay is no longer an option.*
- *Silence is no longer safe.*

FINAL TRUTH OF THE CHAPTER:

This chapter ends with a haunting image:

- A storm outside
- A prophet inside
- The prophet waking up

Because God is about to teach Jonah—*and us*—that storms are invitations to surrender, not signals to escape.

And remember: *One Book of Jonah is enough.*

– 4 –

THROWN OVERBOARD BY THE WILL OF GOD

SURRENDER ISN'T OPTIONAL

Jonah 1:11–16 (NIV) reveals the terror onboard the ship when the storm brought about by Jonah's disregard for God's instruction hits with full force:

> *"The sea was getting rougher and rougher. So they asked him, 'What should we do to you to make the sea calm down for us?'*

"12 'Pick me up and throw me into the sea,' he replied, 'and it will become calm. I know that it is my fault that this great storm has come upon you.'

"13 Instead, the men did their best to row back to land. But they could not, for the sea grew even wilder than before. 14 Then they cried out to the Lord, 'Please, Lord, do not let us die for taking this man's life. Do not hold us accountable for killing an innocent man, for you, Lord, have done as you pleased.' 15 Then they took Jonah and threw him overboard, and the raging sea grew calm. 16 At this the men greatly feared the Lord, and they offered a sacrifice to the Lord and made vows to him."

THERE COMES A MOMENT
WHEN EXPOSURE IS MERCY

Jonah has been confronted. The storm has spoken. The questions have been asked. The lot has fallen.

And now Jonah does something rare ...

... and necessary.

He tells the truth.

"For my sake this great tempest is upon you."

This is the turning point of the story.

- Before repentance is prayer.
- *Before restoration is honesty.*
- Before calm is confession.

God will not heal what we refuse to own.

SURRENDER IS NOT ALWAYS
GENTLE

Jonah does not say ...

"*Let's talk this through.*"

He says ...

"*Throw me overboard.*"

This is not drama ...

... this is surrender.

Some moments in life cannot be negotiated. They must be released.

There are times when the only way forward is down—not into destruction, but into dependence.

You don't always walk out of rebellion ...

... sometimes you fall out of it.

GOD WILL REMOVE YOU TO SAVE OTHERS

The sailors didn't want to throw Jonah overboard.

- They tried harder.
- *They rowed longer.*
- They resisted the solution.

But nothing changed until Jonah was removed.

Here is a hard truth: Sometimes God allows separation—not as punishment, but as protection.

- Not everyone can survive your season of disobedience.
- *Not everyone can afford your delay.*

And God loves the ship too much to let it sink for one passenger.

WHEN YOU LET GO, PEACE RETURNS

The moment Jonah hits the water, the storm stops.

- No gradual calm.
- No slow fade.

Rather, there is *instant peace.*

That tells us something profound: The storm was not about the sea. It was about Jonah.

What you release determines what God resolves.

When Jonah let go of control, God let go of the storm.

THE SEA OBEYED—JONAH DIDN'T

The irony is unmistakable.

- The sea obeys God.
- *The wind obeys God.*
- The storm obeys God.

But the prophet had to be forced. Jonah wasn't willing to follow God without coercion.

Creation responded faster than "the called." And yet—God still pursues Jonah.

- Because calling is not canceled by resistance.
- *Assignment is not revoked by delay.*
- Purpose is not erased by rebellion.

SURRENDER CONVERTS SPECTATORS

Watch what happens next:

- The sailors fear the Lord.
- *They offer sacrifices.*
- They make vows.

Jonah never preached—yet revival broke out.

Even in disobedience, God used Jonah's surrender to reveal Himself.

When you finally let go, others often see God more clearly.

FALLING IS NOT FAILING WHEN GOD IS IN IT

It seems like things cannot get any worse.

- Jonah sinks.
- *The sea closes.*
- The silence deepens.

From the outside ...

... it looks like the end.

But this fall is not fatal ...

... it is formative.

- God is not finished.
- God is positioning Jonah for mercy disguised as confinement.

Sometimes being thrown overboard is the first step back into God's will.

A WORD FOR TODAY

Some of us are fighting storms God intends to end—but only after we release what we're holding onto.

- You don't need a new ship.
- *You don't need a new direction.*
- You need a clean surrender.

Because peace doesn't come from rowing harder ...

... it comes from letting go.

THE QUIET BEFORE THE MIRACLE

Chapter 4 ends with Jonah sinking—and heaven preparing something unseen.

What looks like loss is actually ...

... *transition.*

What feels like the end is actually ...

... *the setup.*

CLOSING TRUTH:

When you finally surrender, God always has something prepared.

It's vital to remember—*one Book of Jonah is enough.*

– 5 –

THE MERCY OF THE FISH

GOD'S PROVISION DOESN'T ALWAYS LOOK LIKE RESCUE

Jonah 1:17 (NIV) gives us one of the most iconic and memorable images from the Word, the tale of the great fish:

> *"Now the Lord provided a huge fish to swallow Jonah, and Jonah was in the belly of the fish three days and three nights."*

WHAT FEELS LIKE JUDGMENT
IS OFTEN PREPARATION

- Jonah hits the water.
- *The storm stops.*
- Silence settles.

And then ...

... the fish.

Let's be clear: *The fish was not punishment. The fish was provision.*

Scripture is intentional again: *"Now the Lord provided a huge fish ..."*

- God did not improvise Jonah's rescue.
- *He did not scramble at the last second.*
- The fish was already on assignment.

Before Jonah surrendered, God had already prepared mercy.

GOD'S RESCUE RARELY LOOKS
LIKE RESCUE

No one would choose this. *No one would pray for this.* No one would design this.

- Darkness
- *Tight quarters*
- No control
- *No audience*
- No exit

Yet this was salvation.

Sometimes God saves you by restricting you. *Sometimes deliverance comes wrapped in discomfort.* Sometimes the answer to your prayer feels like confinement.

God will trap you to keep you.

THE FISH DID WHAT JONAH WOULDN'T

The irony deepens.

Jonah ran from God ... *the fish obeyed God.*

Jonah went where God told him not to ... *the fish went where God sent it.*

Creation keeps outperforming the prophet.

Yet God entrusts Jonah—not the fish—with the message.

Why?

Because calling is about grace, not performance.

ISOLATION IS A GIFT WHEN PRIDE IS LOUD

The belly of the fish removes everything Jonah leaned on:

- No pulpit
- *No reputation*
- No escape
- *No distractions*

No one to impress ... no one to blame.

Just Jonah ...

    ... *and God.*

Some conversations only happen in isolation. *Some lessons require silence.* Some pride only dies in the dark.

God will isolate you to recalibrate you.

YOU CAN'T RUN FOREVER— EVENTUALLY YOU PRAY

- Jonah did not pray on the ship.
- Jonah did not pray in the storm.
- *Jonah prayed in the fish.*

"*From inside the fish Jonah prayed to the Lord his God*" (Jonah 2:1).

It's amazing how clarity comes when options disappear.

When there's no plan B, prayer becomes sincere.

- Not polished
- *Not public*
- Not performative

Prayer becomes desperate. In that moment, it becomes honest and broken.

THE BELLY IS NOT THE END—
IT'S THE CLASSROOM

Jonah thinks he's buried. But he's being taught.

- This is not a tomb.
- This is a *training room*.

God is not trying to silence Jonah. *God is trying to shape him.*

- The fish is not about punishment.
- It's about *preparation for Nineveh*.

Because a prophet who hasn't been broken *will never preach mercy correctly.*

TIME FEELS LONGER WHEN
YOU'RE RESISTING GOD

Three days. Three nights.

- Long enough to think
- *Long enough to feel*
- Long enough to repent

God rarely rushes this stage.

Because rushing transformation usually produces temporary obedience.

God is more interested in who you become than how fast you move.

A WORD FOR THE READER

Some of us are angry at the fish—*when we should be grateful for it.*

You're alive because of the thing you resented. You're still here because of the season you didn't understand. You were preserved by what felt like confinement.

- That relationship ending ...
- *That door closing ...*
- That forced pause ...
- *That interruption ...*

It wasn't rejection ...

... *it was mercy.*

MERCY THAT SMELLS LIKE FISH

The fish is not glamorous.

- It doesn't smell like victory.
- It doesn't look like favor.

But it keeps Jonah alive.

- Sometimes grace smells bad.
- *Sometimes mercy is uncomfortable.*
- Sometimes salvation leaves residue.

But it works.

CLOSING TRUTH:

If God has you in a tight place, don't curse it too quickly.

You might be alive because of it.

- The fish is not the failure.
- The fish is the favor.

And keep this in mind—*one Book of Jonah is enough.*

– 6 –

Prayers from the Belly

WHEN THEOLOGY BECOMES DESPERATION

When the prophet reaches the bottom, he can only look up. We read where Jonah has a change of heart in Jonah 2:1–9 (NIV):

"From inside the fish Jonah prayed to the Lord his God. ² He said: 'In my distress I called to the Lord, and he answered me. From deep in the realm of the dead I called for help, and you listened to my

cry. *3 You hurled me into the depths, into the very heart of the seas, and the currents swirled about me; all your waves and breakers swept over me.*

"4 I said, "I have been banished from your sight; yet I will look again toward your holy temple." 5 The engulfing waters threatened me, the deep surrounded me; seaweed was wrapped around my head. 6 To the roots of the mountains I sank down; the earth beneath barred me in forever. But you, Lord my God, brought my life up from the pit.

"7 When my life was ebbing away, I remembered you, Lord, and my prayer rose to you, to your holy temple. 8 Those who cling to worthless idols turn away from God's love for them. 9 But I, with shouts of grateful praise, will sacrifice to

you. What I have vowed I will make good. I will say, "Salvation comes from the Lord.""

SOME PRAYERS ARE ONLY PRAYED IN THE DARK

- Jonah did not pray on the boat.
- *He did not pray in the storm.*
- He did not pray when the sailors were panicking.

He prayed when he had no control left.

The belly of the fish becomes Jonah's prayer closet.

- No music
- *No altar*
- No audience

Just desperation.

Some prayers don't rise from faith ...

... they rise from survival.

WHEN YOU'RE TRAPPED, THEOLOGY GETS HONEST

Jonah's prayer is not poetic at first.

It is raw.

- "I cried by reason of mine affliction ..."
- *"All thy billows and thy waves passed over me ..."*
- "The waters compassed me about, even to the soul ..."

This is not sermon language. *This is soul language.*

The fish stripped Jonah of his polished spirituality.

Because God is not impressed by eloquence— *He responds to truth.*

JONAH PRAYED ... BUT HE STILL HAD ISSUES

Let's be honest.

Jonah repents of running ...

... but not yet of resentment.

He acknowledges God's power ...

... but not God's compassion for Nineveh.

This prayer is sincere but incomplete ...

... and God still responds.

God answers honest prayers, even when the heart isn't fully healed yet.

That's mercy.

THE BELLY TEACHES YOU
WHO GOD REALLY IS

Jonah's prayer is saturated with Scripture.

- He remembers the Psalms.
- *He remembers the temple.*
- He remembers covenant.

Isolation reactivated memory.

When noise fades ... truth gets louder.

Sometimes God removes your surroundings to restore your remembering.

YOU DON'T PRAY YOUR WAY
OUT—YOU SURRENDER YOUR
WAY OUT

Notice something crucial: *Jonah does not pray for the fish to spit him out.*

He prays for alignment with God before he desires deliverance from his situation.

"Salvation is of the LORD."

That's the breakthrough line.

Until Jonah stopped asking for escape and started declaring surrender, nothing changed.

Deliverance follows alignment—not negotiation.

OBEDIENCE IS THE END OF
THE PRAYER

Jonah says: *"But I, with shouts of grateful praise, will sacrifice to you. What I have vowed I will make good. I will say, 'Salvation comes from the Lord.'"*

This is repentance ...

... *with intention.*

Prayer that does not end in obedience ...

... *is only emotional release.*

God is not after catharsis ...

... *He is after commitment.*

GOD WAITS FOR THE LAST WORD

This next part is powerful, and it reorders our view of how God works:

"And the Lord commanded the fish, and it vomited Jonah onto dry land" (v. 10).

Notice, God didn't speak to the fish until Jonah *spoke correctly to God.*

Heaven was waiting on Jonah's *alignment with God's will.*

When your words line up with God's will, *creation gets new instructions.*

VOMITED—BUT DELIVERED

- Jonah doesn't emerge dignified.
- *He doesn't step out clean.*
- He doesn't walk out to applause.

He is vomited from the belly of the fish.

Grace is not always graceful.

- But he is alive.
- *He is restored.*
- He is repositioned.

A WORD FOR THE READER

Some of you are praying for change ... but God is waiting for surrender.

You want relief ... God wants realignment.

You want out ... God wants you right.

And the moment you say, "Salvation is of the Lord," *the process shifts.*

CLOSING TRUTH:

The belly didn't break Jonah—*it brought him back.*

Prayer didn't change God's mind—*it changed Jonah's posture.*

And when alignment happens, deliverance is never far behind.

Because we hold to this knowledge—*one Book of Jonah is enough.*

– 7 –

VOMITED BACK INTO PURPOSE

SECOND CHANCES ARE RESUMPTIONS

Jonah 2:10–3:1 (NIV) is where God returns to his original instruction to the errant prophet, and it isn't pretty:

> *"And the Lord commanded the fish, and it vomited Jonah onto dry land. Then the word of the Lord came to Jonah a second time ..."*

SECOND CHANCES ARE NOT SOFT RESETS

Jonah does not emerge from the fish refreshed. He is not restored gently. He is expelled.

Grace doesn't always come with dignity. Sometimes restoration is:

- Messy
- *Public*
- Humbling

But it is still restoration.

God would rather restore you raw than leave you lost.

GOD BRINGS YOU BACK TO THE SAME WORD

This may be the most sobering line in the book:

"Then the word of the Lord came to Jonah a

second time ..."

- Not a new assignment
- *Not a revised calling*
- Not a softened version

The same word.

God did not say, *"Jonah, let's try something easier."*

He said, *"Go to Nineveh."*

God does not rewrite obedience ...

... He repeats it.

MERCY IS NOT A LOOPHOLE

Grace gave Jonah another chance, *not another option.*

Too many people think mercy means exemption.

But mercy means re-engagement.

God forgives rebellion, *but He does not reward avoidance.*

Second chances are not escape routes ...

... they are return paths.

DELIVERANCE DOES NOT CANCEL RESPONSIBILITY

- Jonah is alive.
- *Jonah is forgiven.*
- Jonah is repositioned.

But Jonah is still responsible.

Being delivered from the fish did not deliver him from Nineveh.

Being saved from consequence does not release you from calling.

THIS TIME, JONAH GOES

Jonah 3:3 says: *"Jonah obeyed the word of the Lord and went to Nineveh."*

- No argument
- *No delay*
- No detour

Obedience comes quicker after pain.

Sometimes the fish doesn't just save you ...

... it teaches you speed.

YOU SMELL LIKE WHERE YOU'VE BEEN

Let's be honest.

Jonah didn't arrive polished. *He likely still smelled like fish.* He carried the residue of his rebellion.

And God still sent him.

God uses people who smell like mercy.

Your past doesn't disqualify you ...

... it authenticates your message.

PURPOSE IS NOT ALWAYS PLEASANT

- Nineveh is large.
- *Nineveh is hostile.*

- Nineveh is undeserving in Jonah's eyes.

But obedience is not about agreement. It's about alignment.

Jonah obeys externally—even though internally, he still struggles.

And God uses him anyway.

A WORD FOR LEADERS

Some of you are waiting to feel ready again. God is waiting for you to move.

Readiness is often a myth. Obedience is the requirement.

You don't need new instructions. You need immediate obedience.

THE SCARS ARE PROOF YOU SURVIVED

Jonah's story didn't end in the fish. It didn't end in the storm.

It restarted in obedience.

The scars didn't disqualify him. They propelled him.

God doesn't waste what you've survived.

CLOSING TRUTH:

God didn't save Jonah to sideline him. He saved him to send him.

The second word wasn't softer ...

... it was clearer.

And Jonah finally understood:

Delayed obedience is still disobedience ...

... but swift obedience opens the future.

Because one Book of Jonah is enough.

– 8 –

PREACHING WITHOUT PASSION

OBEDIENCE DOESN'T EQUATE PASSION

Jonah 3:4–5 (NIV) shows Jonah in action: *"Jonah began by going a day's journey into the city, proclaiming, 'Forty more days and Nineveh will be overthrown.' 5 The Ninevites believed God. A fast was proclaimed, and all of them, from the greatest to the least, put on sackcloth."*

YOU CAN OBEY GOD WITHOUT LIKING HIS ASSIGNMENT

- Jonah obeys.
- *He goes.*
- He preaches.

But his heart isn't in it.

- There is no joy in his voice.
- *No compassion in his tone.*
- No urgency in his spirit.

His sermon is eight words long in Hebrew.

- No altar call
- *No invitation*
- No appeal

Just judgment. And yet, revival breaks out.

God's power is not limited by the preacher's enthusiasm.

GOD HONORS OBEDIENCE EVEN WHEN THE HEART IS LAGGING

Jonah gives the *bare minimum*. God gives *maximum mercy*.

Jonah announces *destruction*. God releases *repentance*.

This reveals something stunning: *God is more committed to His people than to His prophet's comfort.*

God will use your *obedience* even while He is still working on your *attitude*.

THE MESSAGE WAS RIGHT— THE MOTIVE WAS WRONG

Jonah's words were true. Nineveh did need to repent. Judgment was coming.

But Jonah wanted *judgment* more than *redemption*.

It is possible to preach truth and still miss God's heart.

Orthodoxy without compassion produces resentment, not revival.

REVIVAL SOMETIMES HAPPENS DESPITE THE MESSENGER

The people believe God.

- They repent.
- *They fast.*
- They cry out.

From the king to the cattle.

And Jonah? He's nowhere in the celebration.

Because success doesn't always feel successful when it doesn't match your expectations.

MINIMAL OBEDIENCE STILL MOVES HEAVEN

This should both *comfort* and *convict* us.

Comfort ...

... because God can still work through us.

Conviction ...

... because God deserves more than our

bare minimum.

Jonah preached *reluctantly*. God responded *extravagantly*.

God does not need your passion ...

... but He desires it.

A WARNING FOR LEADERS

It is possible to:

- Preach correctly
- *Serve faithfully*
- Lead effectively

And still resent the people God loves.

- Ministry can become mechanical.
- *Assignments can become burdens.*
- People can become problems.

And if we're not careful ...

... we'll obey externally while resisting internally.

GOD CARES MORE ABOUT
RESULTS THAN REPUTATION

Jonah wanted to look prophetic. *God wanted to save people.*

Jonah wanted to be right. *God wanted to be redemptive.*

Revival embarrassed Jonah's theology of vengeance.

THE CITY RESPONDED FASTER
THAN THE PROPHET

Nineveh repented immediately. Jonah still struggled.

Sometimes the people you judge respond faster than the people who preach.

That should humble us.

CLOSING TRUTH:

Obedience got Jonah to Nineveh, but *compassion was still missing.*

God used Jonah's voice, but Jonah hadn't yet *learned God's heart.*

And that tension sets the stage for the most uncomfortable lesson of all.

Because *one Book of Jonah* is enough—but Jonah still isn't finished.

– 9 –

WHEN REVIVAL OFFENDS THE PROPHET

WHEN GOD SAVES THE PEOPLE YOU WROTE OFF

Jonah 4:1–3 (NIV) reveals Jonah's response to God's redemption of Nineveh:

"But to Jonah this seemed very wrong, and he became angry. ² He prayed to the Lord, 'Isn't this what I said, Lord, when I was still at home? That is what I tried to forestall by fleeing to Tarshish. I knew

that you are a gracious and compassionate God, slow to anger and abounding in love, a God who relents from sending calamity. ³ *Now, Lord, take away my life, for it is better for me to die than to live."'*

SUCCESS CAN REVEAL WHAT FAILURE HID

Jonah's sermon worked.

- The city repented.
- *Judgment was delayed.*
- Mercy triumphed.

And Jonah was furious.

Nothing exposes the heart like answered prayer—especially when God answers it in a way you didn't want.

Failure tests obedience. Success tests alignment.

JONAH DIDN'T FEAR FAILURE—HE FEARED MERCY

Jonah tells God exactly why he ran in the first place:

"I knew that you are a gracious and compassionate God, slow to anger and abounding in love ..."

That is a confession—but *not a compliment.*

Jonah wasn't afraid Nineveh wouldn't repent. He was afraid they *would.*

Jonah didn't doubt God's power ...

... he resented God's compassion.

THE MOST DANGEROUS ANGER IS RELIGIOUS ANGER

Jonah's anger wasn't carnal. It was theological.

He was angry on principle.

- He believed Nineveh deserved judgment.

- *He believed mercy was misplaced.*
- He believed God was being too kind.

When righteousness loses compassion, it becomes cruelty.

Religious anger is dangerous because it feels justified.

WHEN GOD BLESSES PEOPLE YOU DON'T LIKE

God saved:

- Israel's enemies
- *Violent oppressors*
- A wicked city

And Jonah couldn't handle it.

This is the real test of grace: Can you rejoice when God is good to people you wouldn't be good to?

If grace offends you, you don't understand grace.

JONAH LOVED HIS MESSAGE MORE THAN THE MISSION

Jonah wanted his prophecy fulfilled—not his audience saved.

He would rather be right than redemptive.

And that reveals a sobering truth:

- You can love preaching more than people.
- *You can love accuracy more than mercy.*
- You can love justice while ignoring compassion.

A PROPHET WHO WANTED TO DIE

Jonah says:

"Now, Lord, take away my life, for it is better for me to die ..."

This isn't depression. *It's defiance.*

Jonah would rather die than watch God bless Nineveh.

When pride is threatened, even mercy can feel unbearable.

GOD RESPONDS WITH A QUESTION, NOT A LECTURE

God doesn't argue. In the next verse, He asks the big question:

"Is it right for you to be angry?"

That question echoes through history.

Is your anger righteous—or is it *wounded pride?*

Is it about truth—or *control?*

Is it about God's glory—or *your comfort?*

A WORD FOR THE CHURCH

We celebrate revival ...

... *until it happens among people we don't approve of.*

We pray for awakening ...

... until God answers it outside our preferences.

God's mercy rarely follows our boundaries.

THE LESSON JONAH DIDN'T WANT:

Jonah preached repentance to Nineveh.

Now God preaches repentance to Jonah.

We can't forget that one Book of Jonah is enough—but *God still wants Jonah's heart.*

– 10 –

A City Repents ...
and a Prophet
Pouts

SUCCESS THAT EXPOSES THE
HEART

Jonah 4:4–5 (NIV) reveals Jonah's poor
attitude:

> "But the Lord replied, 'Is it right for you
> to be angry?'

> "Jonah had gone out and sat down at a
> place east of the city. There he made

himself a shelter, sat in its shade and
waited to see what would happen to the
city."

YOU CAN BE NEAR REVIVAL AND STILL BE FAR FROM GOD'S HEART

Jonah leaves the city ...

... but not the situation.

He positions himself *just close enough* to watch, but *far enough* to avoid participation.

- He builds a booth.
- *He finds shade.*
- He waits.

Not to rejoice ...

... but to see if judgment from God might still fall.

Jonah didn't leave God ...

... he left compassion.

WAITING ON GOD FOR THE WRONG OUTCOME

Jonah is hoping mercy will fail.

That's uncomfortable to admit—but it's true.

He obeyed publicly, but now he waits privately for God to *undo what grace has done.*

This is the tension of the chapter:

Jonah wants God's power without God's patience.

THE BOOTH OF BITTERNESS

Jonah builds his own shelter.

This is important.

When you step out of alignment, you start constructing substitutes:

- Self-protection
- *Emotional distance*
- Spiritual excuses

Jonah's booth is not shelter—*it's separation.*

What you build to protect yourself can become the place you isolate yourself.

WATCHING FOR FIRE WHILE SURROUNDED BY MERCY

Jonah watches Nineveh like a critic, not a shepherd.

He is waiting for fire, while repentance is already burning.

He wants destruction, while God wants transformation.

It's possible to sit in the presence of a miracle and still root for disaster.

GOD LETS JONAH SIT

This may be the most gracious part of the chapter.

- God doesn't force Jonah back into the city.
- *God doesn't strike him.*

- God lets him sit.

Because sometimes God allows us to linger in our wrong posture so we can finally see it clearly.

PROXIMITY DOES NOT EQUAL ALIGNMENT

Jonah is geographically close to Nineveh but *spiritually distant.*

He is near the move of God but *untouched by it.*

That's a warning for leaders:

You can be close to revival and still not rejoice.

You can witness repentance and still resent it.

GOD IS ABOUT TO TEACH JONAH AGAIN

Jonah thinks the lesson is over ...

... but God is not finished teaching.

Because Jonah still values:

- His comfort over compassion
- *His perspective over God's purpose*
- His booth over broken people

And God is about to use something small to expose something big.

A Quiet Setup:

This chapter ends quietly.

- No storm
- No fish
- No fire

Just a prophet sitting, waiting, watching, and missing the miracle.

But heaven is preparing the next object lesson, because Jonah still hasn't learned the final truth:

God cares more about people than postures.

And remember—**one Book of Jonah is enough**.

THE GOD WHO ASKS QUESTIONS

IS IT RIGHT FOR YOU TO BE ANGRY?

Jonah 4:6–7 (NIV) gives us God's plan for Jonah's turnaround:

> *"Then the Lord God provided a leafy plant and made it grow up over Jonah to give shade for his head to ease his discomfort, and Jonah was very happy about the plant. 7 But at dawn the next day God provided a worm, which chewed the plant so that it withered."*

GOD STILL PREPARES—EVEN WHEN WE POUT

This verse is stunning.

- Jonah is angry.
- *Jonah is sulking.*
- Jonah is spiritually out of alignment.

And God still prepares.

> *"The LORD God provided a leafy plant ..."*

The same language is used for:

- The fish
- *The storm*
- The city

God has not stopped being God just because Jonah stopped being grateful.

God's kindness is not dependent on your attitude.

GOD KNOWS WHAT WILL REVEAL YOUR HEART

- The plant grows fast.
- *The shade is immediate.*
- The relief is real.

And Jonah is exceedingly glad.

The same man who was angry about a city repenting is joyful over a plant growing.

That contrast is intentional.

Jonah rejoices over comfort more than compassion. *What makes you glad reveals what you value.*

TEMPORARY BLESSINGS EXPOSE PERMANENT PRIORITIES

- The plant did not preach.
- *The plant did not repent.*
- The plant did not cry out.

But Jonah loved it.

Why? Because it benefited him.

This is not about *botany*. It's about *misplaced affection*.

Jonah had more emotion for his shade than for a city of souls.

GOD USES COMFORT BEFORE CORRECTION

God didn't start with confrontation.

He started with kindness, because *grace often precedes exposure.*

God lets Jonah enjoy the plant before He takes it away—not to be cruel, but to teach.

God often gives you what you want temporarily to show you what you love ultimately.

THE DANGER OF SELECTIVE JOY

Jonah is happy when:

- He is comfortable.
- *He is shaded.*
- He is relieved.

But angry when:

- Others are spared.
- *Enemies are forgiven.*
- Mercy is extended.

That's selective joy.

And selective joy reveals a selective heart.

GOD IS TEACHING JONAH
ABOUT PERSPECTIVE

The plant came quickly. The plant felt essential. The plant seemed important.

But it was never permanent.

Jonah mistook provision for priority.

Not everything that helps you is meant to rule you.

A WORD FOR LEADERS

God still provides for us—even when we're sulking.

But that provision can become a mirror.

If the loss of comfort devastates you more than the loss of people concerns you, your priorities are out of alignment.

GOD'S QUESTIONS ARE INVITATIONS

God is not setting Jonah up to fail. He is inviting Jonah to see himself.

The question hasn't come yet—*but it's coming.*

Because God doesn't shame—*He asks.*

And the questions of God are designed to heal what lectures never could.

CLOSING THOUGHT:

The same God who prepared the fish now prepares a plant.

- One to save Jonah's life.
- One to expose Jonah's heart.

Both are mercy.

And Jonah is about to learn that comfort is not the goal—*compassion is.*

Because

one book of

Jonah ...

... *is enough.*

– 12 –

The Plant, the Worm, and the Wind

TEMPORARY COMFORTS GOD ALLOWS AND REMOVES

Jonah 4:7–8 (NIV) sets Jonah up for a revelation from God:

"But at dawn the next day God provided a worm, which chewed the plant so that it withered. ⁸ When the sun rose, God provided a scorching east wind, and the sun blazed on Jonah's head so that he

grew faint. He wanted to die, and said, 'It would be better for me to die than to live.'"

THE SAME GOD WHO GIVES ALSO TAKES AWAY

This chapter dismantles every shallow version of faith.

The same God who prepared the *plant*, now prepares the *worm* and the *wind*.

Three preparations. *One lesson.*

God is sovereign over provision *and* removal.

God does not just bless—He teaches.

THE WORM WAS SMALL—BUT THE LESSON WAS BIG

The worm is almost laughable.

- No storm
- *No fish*

- No drama

Just a small, unseen creature silently undoing Jonah's comfort.

God does not always use big things to correct us. Sometimes He uses:

- Small irritations
- Slow losses
- Quiet removals

What you idolize, God will gently dismantle.

JONAH DIDN'T LOSE HIS CALLING—HE LOST HIS COMFORT

Notice what God removes:

- Not Jonah's life
- *Not Jonah's purpose*
- Not Jonah's future

Just the shade.

God is not punishing Jonah. He is *exposing him.*

Jonah was more attached to *relief* than to *righteousness*.

THEN CAME THE WIND

As if the worm weren't enough, God prepares the wind.

- Heat
- *Pressure*
- Exhaustion

Jonah is overwhelmed.

The same prophet who endured a storm at sea now collapses under sunshine.

What you can't endure often reveals what you're clinging to.

JONAH IS ANGRY AGAIN

Jonah says—*again*—that he would rather die.

But listen closely: Jonah is not *angry about injustice*.

He is *angry about inconvenience.*

When *comfort* left, so did his *composure.*

GOD ASKS THE FINAL QUESTION

"Is it right for you to be angry about the plant?" (v. 9a).

This is surgical.

God narrows the issue.

- No Nineveh
- *No theology*
- No enemies

Just a plant.

And Jonah answers honestly from his anger, revealing his heart:

"It is,' he said. 'And I'm so angry I wish I were dead'" (v. 9b).

That's the confession. Jonah admits it:

He cares more about a plant than about people.

THE REVELATION JONAH DIDN'T WANT

God responds with perspective:

- You cared about a plant you didn't plant.
- *You labored for nothing that grew overnight.*
- You mourned what was temporary.

And then God delivers the final truth:

"And should I not have concern for the great city of Nineveh?" (v. 11).

God is saying: *"If you can care about temporary comfort, why can't I care about eternal souls?"*

COMFORT IS NEVER THE STANDARD

God never promised Jonah *comfort*. He promised Jonah *purpose*.

The plant was *temporary*. The people were

eternal.

Jonah chose *shade.* God chose *souls.*

Whenever comfort and compassion compete, compassion always wins with God.

THE BOOK ENDS WITH A QUESTION

- No resolution
- *No response from Jonah*
- No neat ending

Because the question isn't just for Jonah—it's for us.

What do you care about most?

Your comfort ...

... or God's compassion?

Final Truth of the Chapter:

God will bless you. God will remove things. God will apply pressure.

Not to harm you—*but to align you.*

Because when comfort becomes your priority, God will lovingly unsettle you until compassion becomes your posture.

And that is why:

One Book of Jonah is definitely enough.

– 13 –

COMPASSION GOD WILL NOT APOLOGIZE FOR

GOD'S MERCY TOWARD PEOPLE WE DON'T LIKE

Jonah 4:9–11 (NIV) reveals God's mercy and compassion for humanity:

"But God said to Jonah, 'Is it right for you to be angry about the plant?'

"'It is,' he said. 'And I'm so angry I wish I were dead.'

"¹⁰ But the Lord said, 'You have been concerned about this plant, though you did not tend it or make it grow. It sprang up overnight and died overnight. ¹¹ And should I not have concern for the great city of Nineveh, in which there are more than a hundred and twenty thousand people who cannot tell their right hand from their left—and also many animals?'"

GOD ENDS WITH WHAT JONAH AVOIDED

The book ends the way Jonah began—with God's heart.

- No miracle
- *No fire*
- No fish

Just compassion.

- God does not explain Himself.
- *God does not justify Himself.*
- God does not soften the truth.

He asks one final question—and then lets it hang.

God refuses to apologize for being merciful.

GOD COUNTS PEOPLE WHOM JONAH COUNTED AS ENEMIES

Jonah saw Nineveh as *wicked*. God saw Nineveh as *people*.

God names them:
- People who don't yet know right from left
- *Families*
- Livestock
- *An entire city worth sparing*

God doesn't minimize Nineveh's sin. He magnifies His mercy.

God sees what you dismiss.

COMPASSION IS NOT WEAKNESS

Jonah believed mercy compromised justice.

God shows otherwise.

God's compassion is not denial of truth—it is *redemption of it.*

Judgment would have been easy. Mercy *required patience.*

It takes more power to redeem than to destroy.

GOD CARES ABOUT WHAT YOU IGNORE

God even mentions the cattle.

Why?

To show the depth of His care.

God's mercy reaches further than Jonah's concern.

If it matters to God, it should matter to us.

GRACE THAT OFFENDS THE RELIGIOUS

Nineveh's salvation was a theological crisis for Jonah.

Because *grace exposed Jonah's limits.*

We celebrate mercy—*until it's given to people we don't think deserve it.*

That's when grace confronts pride.

THE BOOK ENDS WITHOUT JONAH'S ANSWER

We never hear Jonah respond, because the real question isn't Jonah's answer. *It's ours.*

Will we align with God's compassion? *Or retreat into comfort and resentment?*

WHY THE STORY STOPS HERE

The book ends abruptly because the lesson is

complete.

Everything that needed to be said has been said.

One Book of Jonah is enough.

God will not write a sequel to explain why mercy matters.

He has already shown us.

A WORD FOR TODAY'S CHURCH

God's compassion still:

- Crosses borders
- *Offends preferences*
- Disrupts comfort
- *Challenges pride*

And God is still asking:

"Should I not have concern for those who need my mercy?"

CLOSING STATEMENT:

- I choose compassion over comfort.
- *I choose obedience over offense.*
- I choose people over preferences.

Because God's mercy saved me—*and I will not resent it saving others.*

And now I understand:

One Book of Jonah is enough.

A CLOSING
PRAYER

Heavenly Father,

Let our hearts be filled with compassion for the lost and the needy.

Let us feel Your broken heart for those who have yet to find their way to You.

Let us cast off our short-sighted self-concern and show Your love to everyone around us.

Let us be Your hand of mercy to the world.

In Jesus' name,
Amen.

A FINAL WORD

You can find Tim on the South Texas District website at www.stxag.org, on Facebook, or at his Houston office when he's not traveling his home state ministering in the churches across the South Texas District.

He'd be thrilled to connect with you and share stories of God's faithfulness.

www.ingramcontent.com/pod-product-compliance
Lightning Source LLC
Chambersburg PA
CBHW070014110426
42741CB00034B/1754